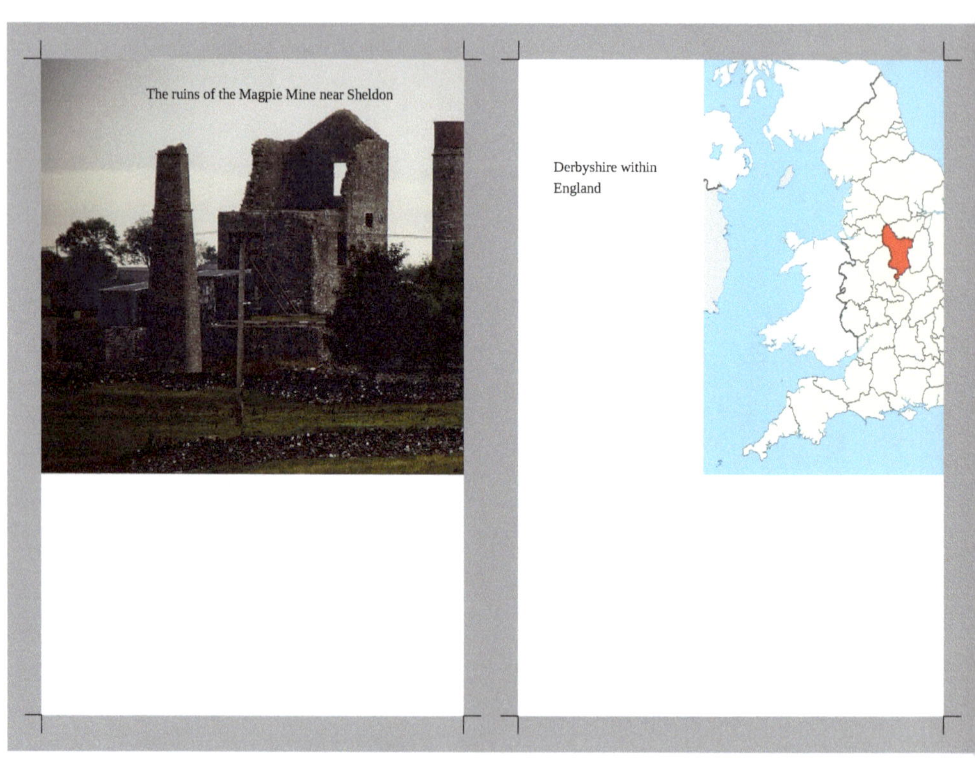

The ruins of the Magpie Mine near Sheldon

Derbyshire within
England

Chatsworth Autumn Bridge Colour Leaves Orange
Ladybower Reservoir Plug Hole Overflow V
Nature

The henge monument at Arbor Low

Derbyshire England Great Britain Sky Clouds Sunset
Ladybower Reservoir Derwent Valley Derbyshire Peak

Ladybower Reservoir Upper Derwent Valley Derbyshire
Derwent Dam Derwent Valley Derbyshire England Flood

Trail Head England English Footpath Co
County Hall, Matlock

Derbyshire England Great Britain
Moorland Moors
Mam Tor High Peak Castleton Derbyshire

Love Locks Bridge Bakewell Bridge Rom
Lock
Belper Derbyshire Peak District River Wei

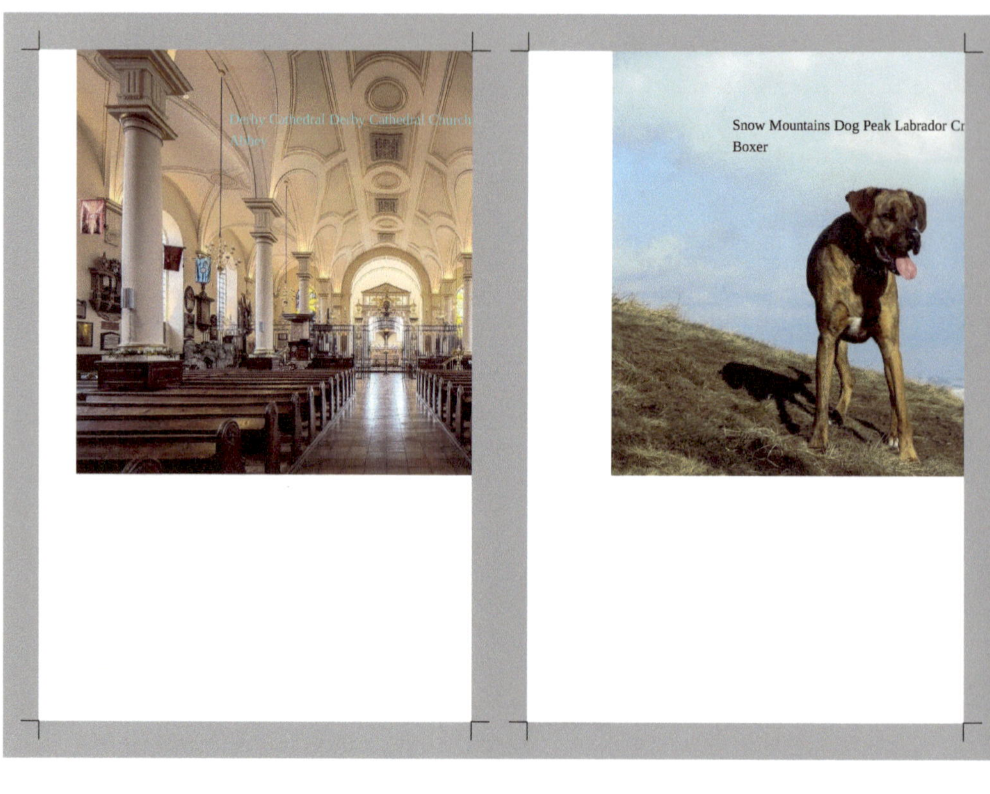
Derby Cathedral Derby Cathedral Church Abbey
Snow Mountains Dog Peak Labrador Cr Boxer

Stonewall Stone Wall Derbyshire Dry Rough Rock
Belper Derbyshire Peak District River M

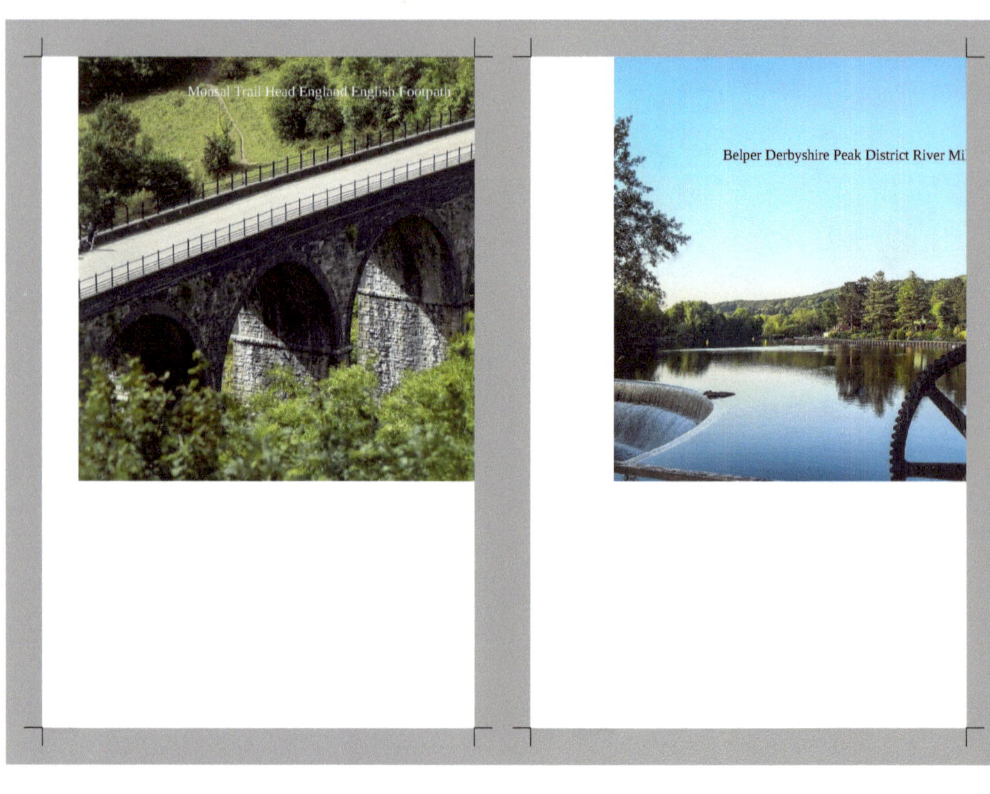
Monsal Trail Head England English Footpath
Belper Derbyshire Peak District River Mill

Drystone Wall Walls Stones Outdoors Uk Derbyshire
Belper Derbyshire Peak District Peak District

Belper Derbyshire Peak District Peak Dis

Moss Greenery Drystone Wall Walls Stones
Outdoors

Oatcakes Derbyshire Oatcakes Bre
The Old Railway Incline Cromford
Middleton Top

The Old Railway Incline Cromford Middleton
Hardwick Hall Stately Home Country Home Architect

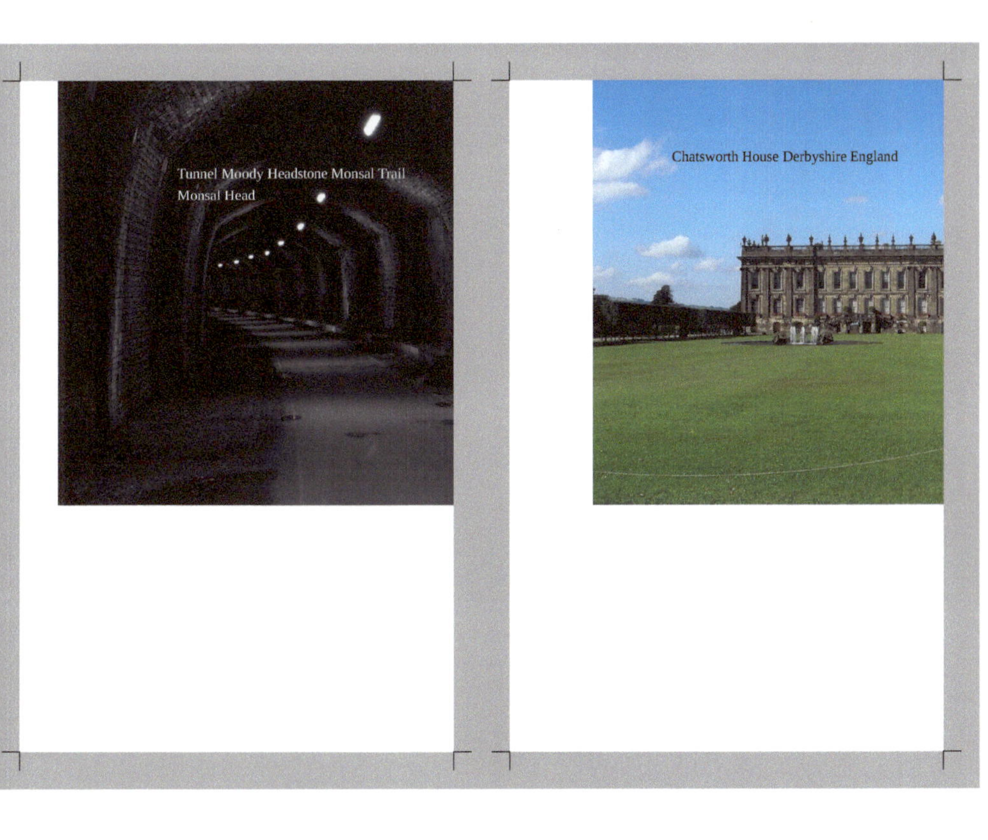

Tunnel Moody Headstone Monsal Trail Monsal Head
Chatsworth House Derbyshire England

Belper Derbyshire Peak District River
Hardwick Hall Hardwick Tudor Architecture Windows

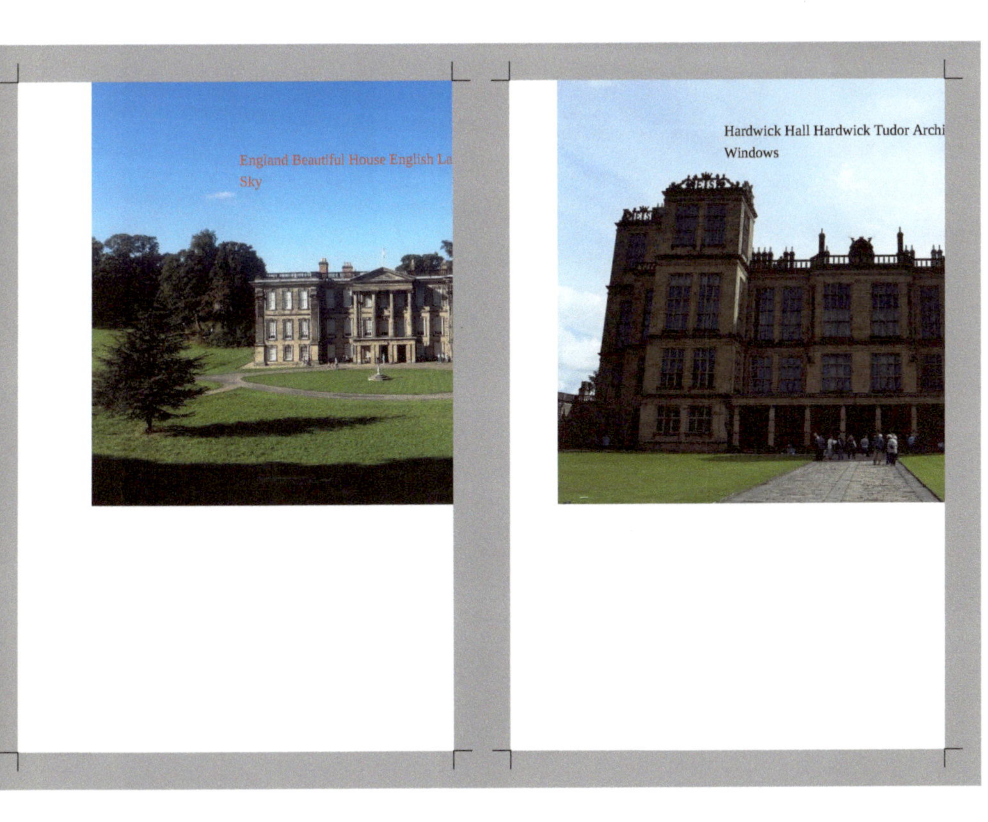
England Beautiful House English La
Sky
Hardwick Hall Hardwick Tudor Archi
Windows

Belper Derbyshire Peak District Peak Di
Belper Derbyshire Peak District Peak District

Chatsworth House England Home Grounds English
Peak District Sunset District Landscape Sk

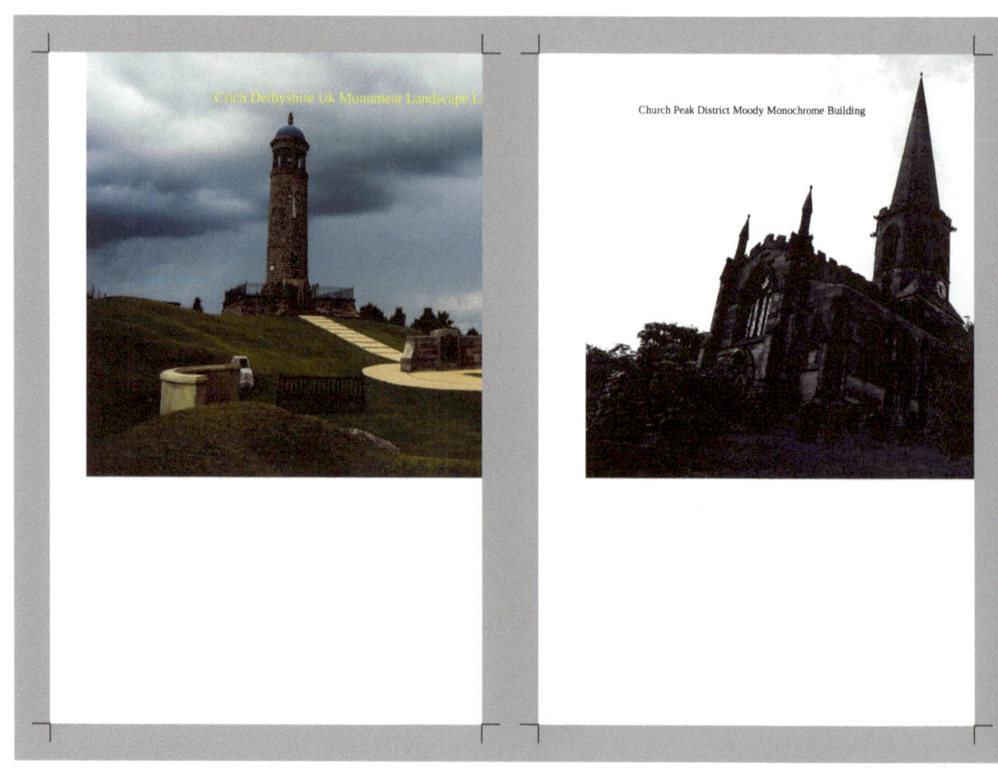

Crich Derbyshire Uk Monument Landscape L

Church Peak District Moody Monochrome Building

Bakewell Derbyshire England District Peak
British
Wall Stone Bakewell Derbyshire England

Bakewell Derbyshire England District Peak British
Calke Abbey Derbyshire National Trust H

Reservoir Tree Derbyshire Scenic
Countryside Rural
Belper Derbyshire Peak District River I

Church Derbyshire Cemetery
Lake District Mountains Landscape C
Rural

Keswick Lake District England Uk Scenic Cumbria
Thorpe Cloud Ilam Dovedale

Moor Field Rural Country Sky Black And White
Roaches Hen Cloud Peak District England National

Peak District Reservoir Ladybower Reservoir
Bridge
Winter Landscape Christmas Snow
December

Natural Rock Formation Sandstone The Roaches
Geology
Peak District Cycling Walks

Nature Panoramic Sky Landscape Sunset The
Cloud
Peak District Reservoir Howden Reservoir Tre
Calm

Peak District Reservoir Howden Reservoir Trees Calm

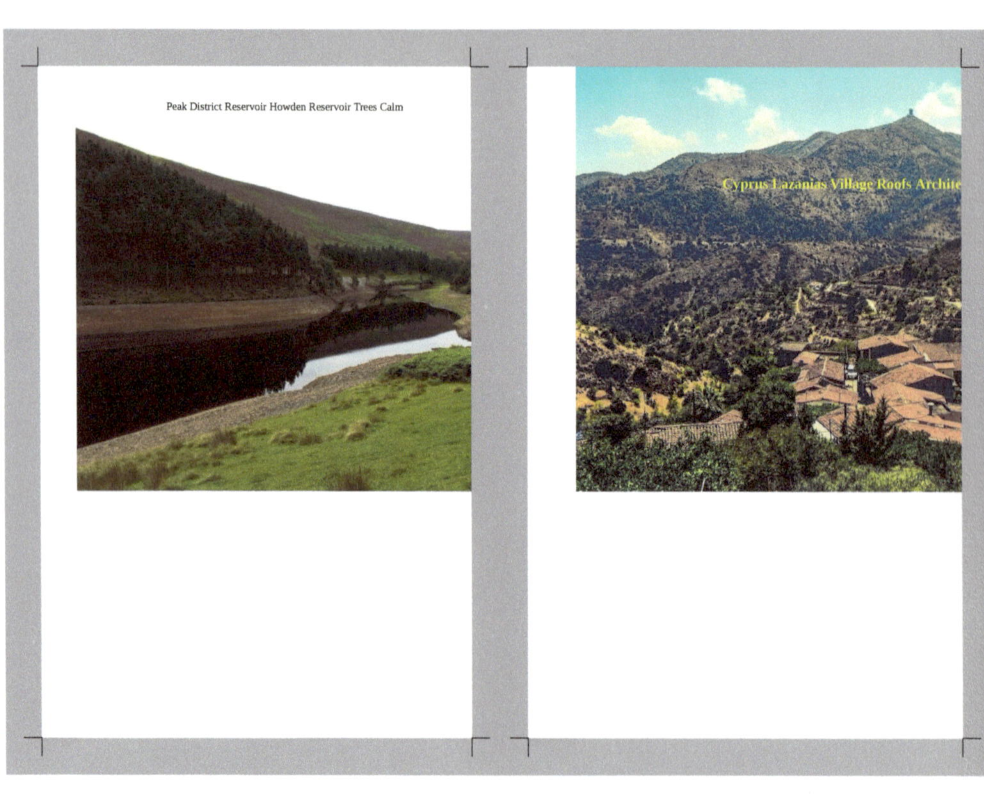

Peak District Reservoir Howden Reservoir Trees Calm
Peak District Reservoir Howden Reservoir Trees Calm

Peak District Reservoir Howden Reservoir Trees Calm
Peak District Reservoir Upper Derwent Reservoir Dam

Cyprus Troodos Mountains Countryside Landscape
Waterfall Peak District Cascade Nature River

Peak District Reservoir Howden Reservoir Dam
Peak District Reservoir Howden Reservoir Dam

Chatsworth House Peak District Grounds Architecture
Chatsworth House Lake Peak District Groun

Peak District Reservoir Ladybower Reservoir Bridge

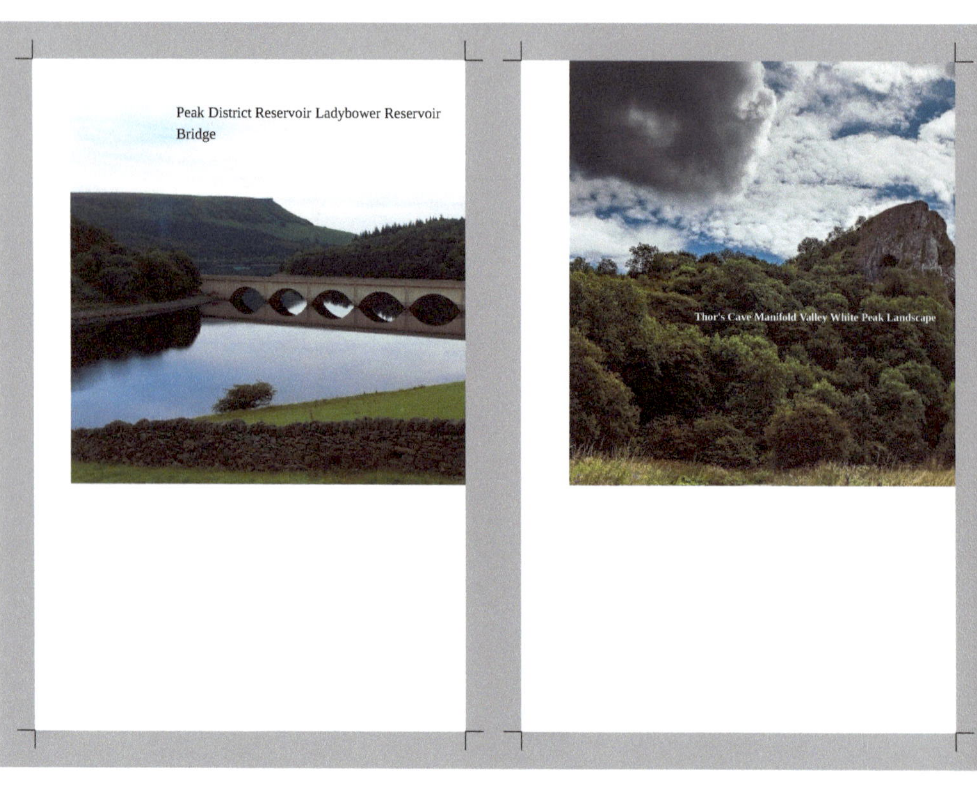

Chatsworth Historic House England Uk
Holme Holmfirth Peak District

Lake District England Mountains Snow Scafe
Pike
Peak District Reservoir Howden Reservoir Dam

Peak District Reservoir Howden Reservoir Dam
Landscape Valley Peak District
Manifold Valley

Cumbria Lake District Gable Hills Lakeland
The Roaches Peak District Winter Snow

Peak District Reservoir Howden Reservoir Trees Calm
Winter Landscape Christmas Snow December

Lake District Mountain English Countryside Lake
Landscape Sheep Sky Horizon Nature Heaven Animal

Peak District Reservoir Howden Reservoir Dam
Tree Rugged Weathered Solitary Peak District

Peak District Reservoir Howden Reservoir Dam

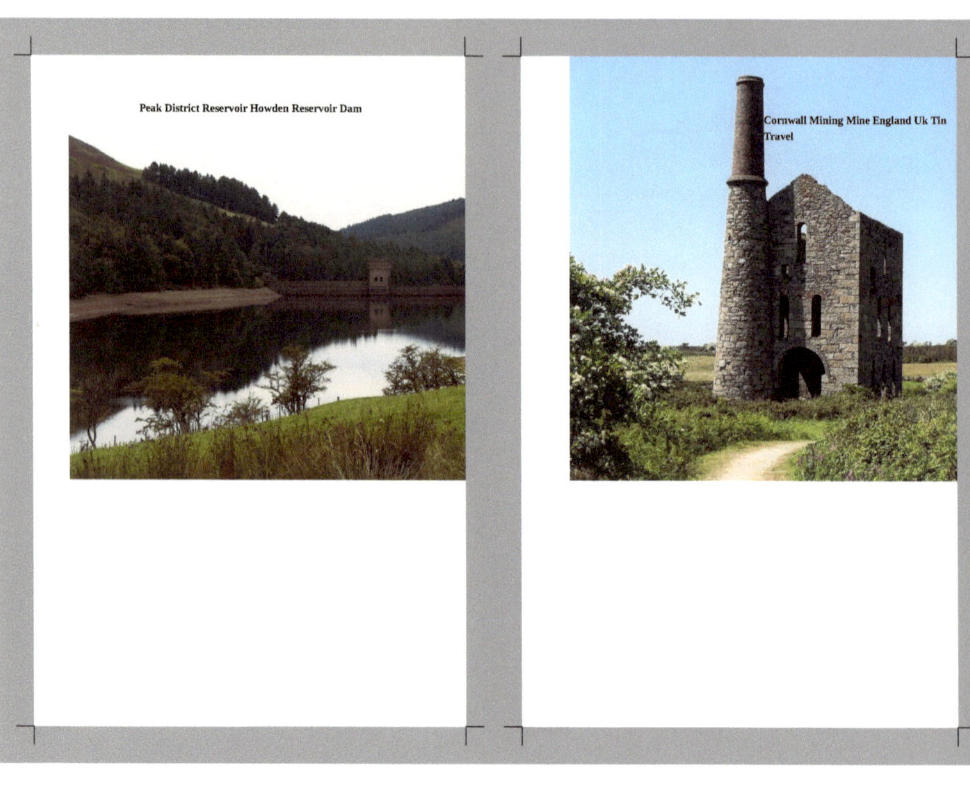

Cornwall Mining Mine England Uk Tin Travel

Clee Hill Radio Transmitter Shropshire Uk
Slate Mine Open Cast Delabole Cornwall Quarry Uk

Mines Cornwall Tin Uk Cornish English Buildin
Aerial View Mines Cornwall Botallack Mining

Proof